It's My State!

SOUTH CAROLINA

The Palmetto State

Debra Hess, William McGeveran, and Laura L. Sullivan

Cavendish Square

New York

Published in 2016 by Cavendish Square Publishing, LLC
243 5th Avenue, Suite 136, New York, NY 10016

Library of Congress Cataloging-in-Publication Data

Hess, Debra.
South Carolina / Debra Hess, William McGeveran, and Laura L. Sullivan.
pages cm. — (It's my state!)
Includes index.
ISBN 978-1-6271-3175-9 (hardcover) — ISBN 978-1-6271-3177-3 (ebook)
1. South Carolina—Juvenile literature. I. McGeveran, William. II. Sullivan, Laura L., 1974- III. Title.

F269.3.H47 2016
975.7—dc23

2015028670

Editorial Director: David McNamara
Editor: Fletcher Doyle
Copy Editor: Rebecca Rohan
Art Director: Jeffrey Talbot
Designer: Stephanie Flecha
Senior Production Manager: Jennifer Ryder-Talbot
Production Editor: Renni Johnson
Photo Research: J8 Media

Printed in the United States of America

SOUTH CAROLINA
CONTENTS

A QUICK LOOK AT

★ State Tree: Sabal Palmetto

This tree has a spongy trunk and large fanlike leaves that can grow longer than 7 feet (2 meters). The sabal **palmetto** played a role in the American Revolution because a fort made from its wood repelled British cannonballs. Part of the tree provides the edible heart of palm, though harvesting kills the tree.

★ State Flower: Yellow Jessamine

Yellow jessamine vines wrap around trees and fences all over the state and are popular additions to gardens. The leaves are green throughout the year. In spring, the bright yellow, trumpet-shaped flowers bloom, symbolizing "constancy in, loyalty to, and patriotism in the service of the state." The flowers are both pretty and poisonous.

★ State Bird: Carolina Wren

The Carolina wren can be found in woods, fields, or swamps. It may build its nest in odd places—even in boxes, flowerpots, or shoes. A wren couple stays together for life. This bird, along with the palmetto and the yellow jessamine, appears on the South Carolina quarter that was issued by the US Mint in 2000.

SOUTH CAROLINA
POPULATION: 4,625,364

★ State Animal: White-tailed Deer

White-tailed deer are often seen in the South Carolina woods. They can run up to 30 miles an hour (50 kilometers per hour). When the deer is alarmed, it may lift up its tail, showing a white underside. This is a warning to nearby deer to be on their guard.

★ State Reptile: Loggerhead Sea Turtle

At the suggestion of a fifth-grade class, loggerheads were named the state reptile in 1988. The adults weigh around 250 pounds (100 kilograms). Every year, the females lay their eggs on beaches. Because their population is endangered, or at risk of dying out, programs have been set up to help protect them.

★ State Dog: Boykin Spaniel

A South Carolina hunter named Whit Boykin bred the first Boykin spaniels one hundred years ago. He needed a dog small enough to fit in a canoe. People still use these stocky, brown spaniels to hunt turkeys, ducks, doves, and pheasants. These dogs also make excellent family pets, being friendly, social, and energetic.

Dorothy Porcher Legge first restored row houses in Charleston's historic district and painted them in Caribbean colors in the 1930s. When others followed her lead, it created the famous Rainbow Row.

The Palmetto State

One of the thirteen original colonies that formed the United States, South Carolina is located in the southeastern United States, along the Atlantic Coast. It stretches some 275 miles (440 kilometers) from the mountains and hills in the west to the seacoast, with its sandy beaches, in the east. It extends some 220 miles (350 km) from north to south.

South Carolina is not a very big state. With a land area of 30,110 square miles (77,983 square kilometers), it is the tenth-smallest state and the smallest state in the Deep South. In population, South Carolina ranks twenty-fourth, or around the middle. The 2010 census reported that 4,625,364 people reside in the state. South Carolina is divided into forty-six counties. The biggest county by area is Horry County, along the coast to the north. This county includes the resort area of Myrtle Beach. Myrtle Beach is known for its beachfront boardwalk, balmy climate, and sand the color of brown sugar.

Spanish explorers arrived in the region in the sixteenth century, and the English settled Charleston, one of the South's oldest and most beautiful cities with its stately mansions, in 1670. In March 1776, the state passed a constitution to set up a government, so it was the first colony to declare its independence from Great Britain. This happened months

The Blue Ridge Mountains bring beauty to the northwest border of South Carolina.

before the Declaration of Independence was signed. During the American Revolution, the tide of the war in the South was turned when the Continental Army won several major battles in the state. In 1788, South Carolina became the eighth state to ratify (approve) the US Constitution. South Carolina **seceded** (withdrew) from the Union in December 1860, the first state to do so. The Civil War began when Confederate troops fired on Union-occupied Fort Sumter, in Charleston Harbor, in April 1861.

The **civil rights** movement helped improve race relations in the state during the 1950s and afterward. Today, the population is growing, and tourism is among many industries adding to the diverse economy. South Carolinians and visitors alike enjoy the state's mild climate and historic and cultural attractions, as well as its forests, parks, gardens, beaches, and golf courses.

South Carolina Borders	
North:	North Carolina
South:	Georgia Atlantic Ocean
East:	Atlantic Ocean
West:	Georgia

The Landscape

South Carolina can be divided into three main geographic regions. They cross the state diagonally in three belts of varying size. The Blue Ridge region occupies the northwest corner, along the border with Georgia and North Carolina. It is the smallest of the three regions. Below it, to the south and east, is a large, hilly region known as the Piedmont. These two belts make up what South Carolinians call the up-country. South and east of the Piedmont is the Atlantic Coastal Plain, which covers around two-thirds of the state. This region is often called the low country.

The Blue Ridge Region

The northwest corner of the state is covered by the Blue Ridge Mountains, which stretch from northern Georgia to southern Pennsylvania. This region of the state contains the highest elevations. They are part of the larger Appalachian mountain system, which runs through much of the eastern part of the United States. Sassafras Mountain, within the Blue Ridge Mountains, rises 3,560 feet (1,085 m) above sea level. This is the state's highest point.

The Blue Ridge region is a scenic area with dense forests and winding streams. The ecosystem in this area is classified as the Appalachian-Blue Ridge Forest **ecoregion**. This area of temperate forests has extremely high biodiversity. This means it is known for having a large number of different species of native animals and plants. Geologically, the area has been stable for a very long time. This has allowed plant and animal species to become firmly established. Also, the ridges and valleys are usually oriented north to south. That allowed species to move south more easily during ice ages and expand north again during warming periods.

A portion of the Sumter National Forest is located in the Blue Ridge region, along with a number of state parks. Caesar's Head State Park, located in Greenville County on the border of North Carolina, is a popular destination for outdoor enthusiasts. The rocky outcrop that gave the park its name doesn't look like a Roman emperor; it was probably named after a hiker's pet dog. Throughout the region there are excellent hiking trails, as well as lakes and rivers ideal for boating or fishing. The Chattooga River, which runs along South Carolina's northwestern border, is popular with white-water rafters.

The Piedmont

The land between the Blue Ridge Mountains and the Atlantic Coastal Plain is called the Piedmont. This region is part of a long line of rolling hills that stretches from New York

SOUTH CAROLINA
COUNTY MAP

SOUTH CAROLINA
POPULATION BY COUNTY

County	Population	County	Population
Abbeville	25,417	Hampton	21,090
Aiken	160,099	Horry	269,291
Allendale	10,419	Jasper	24,777
Anderson	187,126	Kershaw	61,697
Bamberg	15,987	Lancaster	76,652
Barnwell	22,621	Laurens	66,537
Beaufort	162,233	Lee	19,220
Berkeley	177,843	Lexington	262,391
Calhoun	15,175	Marion	33,062
Charleston	350,209	Marlboro	28,933
Cherokee	55,342	McCormick	10,233
Chester	33,140	Newberry	37,508
Chesterfield	46,734	Oconee	74,273
Clarendon	34,971	Orangeburg	92,501
Colleton	38,892	Pickens	119,224
Darlington	68,681	Richland	384,504
Dillon	32,062	Saluda	19,875
Dorchester	136,555	Spartanburg	284,307
Edgefield	26,985	Sumter	107,456
Fairfield	23,956	Union	28,961
Florence	136,885	Williamsburg	34,423
Georgetown	60,158	York	226,073
Greenville	451,225		
Greenwood	69,661		

Source: US Bureau of the Census, 2010

Woodland trails pass through Caesars Head State Park in Greenville County near the North Carolina border.

to Alabama. It is the remnant of an old mountain chain that has been worn down to hills by erosion and time. The word piedmont comes from a French word meaning "foothill." In South Carolina, the hills of the Piedmont can measure from around 200 feet (60 m) to more than 1,000 feet (300 m) above sea level. The Piedmont also has forests, lakes, and fast-flowing rivers and streams.

The land in the Piedmont is often thin and stony, and not the best land for farming. It has been further depleted of nutrients by a history of cotton farming. Although many people have practiced agriculture there despite these obstacles, today much of the region has been planted with loblolly pine trees that are grown for their **timber**.

Atlantic Seaboard Fall Line

To the east of the Piedmont is an area known as the Atlantic Seaboard Fall Line. This is a boundary between the mountainous area and the sandy coastal area. Beyond the fall line, rivers begin flowing down toward the ocean. Power produced by the downhill rushing of water has historically been put to use in grist and textile mills. Today, it is used

Many waterfalls tumble out of the mountains of the Blue Ridge.

for **hydroelectric** power. The prosperity brought about by these mills has helped many South Carolina cities grow. Areas east of the fault line also had an easier time conducting trade because the rivers could be easily navigated up to the fall line.

Atlantic Coastal Plain

Between the coastal plain and the Piedmont is the Sandhills Region. Millions of years ago, when the ocean levels were much higher, this area was South Carolina's coast. Now, only the eroded sandy hills remain of what was once a long coastline. The sandhills rise as high as 600 feet (180 m). The state capital, Columbia, lies in these hills.

The natural environment of the Sandhills Region consists of pine and scrub oak. Wildfires, logging, and poor farming methods nearly ruined the area's timber industry and caused wildlife to leave. In the 1960s, the area was used as a model for forest management. A program of setting controlled fires reduced wildfires, helped restore native longleaf pines, and increased growth of plants eaten by wildlife. Habitats improved, and wildlife returned to the area. The dry, sandy soil isn't suited for most agriculture. Beyond the sandhills lie the pine barrens, and farther east is the true coastline of the Atlantic Coastal Plain. This geographic region stretches from New York to Florida, and it includes the area around the Chesapeake Bay. The coastal plain in South Carolina can be divided into three distinct regions.

More than 60 miles (about 100 km) of the coastline in the north is made up of white, or light brown, sandy beaches known as the Grand Strand. It runs from Winyah Bay to the Little River. Millions of tourists visit the Grand Strand's beaches every year. The hotspot is Myrtle Beach, which attracts huge numbers of tourists each season for its theme parks, restaurants, shopping, and musical venues.

Hilton Head Island is one of the most popular tourist destinations in South Carolina.

South along the coast is the Santee River **delta** region. Two channels of this river empty into the Atlantic Ocean. Together, they create the largest river delta on the east coast of the United States. There are an estimated 400,000 acres (161,874 hectares) of marshes and 100,000 acres (40,469 ha) of tidal swamps, all teeming with life, in the low country.

The Sea Islands are a chain of more than one hundred barrier islands that extend along much of the state's Atlantic Coast, from the Santee River in South

★ 10 ★ KEY SITES ★ ★ ★

Carolina Opry

Congaree National Park

Fort Sumter
National Monument

1. Carolina Opry

This country music extravaganza in Myrtle Beach was named Most Outstanding Attraction by the South Carolina Department of Parks, Recreation, and Tourism. It also received the Governor's Cup, the state's highest tourism award.

2. Congaree National Park

This national park near Eastover is on the Congaree River. Visitors can experience the amazing biodiversity of the area on hiking paths or canoe trails. The park has many national and state champion trees remarkable for their height or girth.

3. Fort Sumter National Monument

Explore Civil War history at three sites in Charleston. Visitors can start at the Educational Center and then take a twenty-minute ferry ride to the original Fort Sumter. Nearby Sullivan's Island is home to Fort Moultrie.

4. Greenville Zoo

Located in Greenville, this zoo's mission focuses on education, conservation, and giving people an appreciation for the natural world. Exhibits feature many primates, red pandas, big cats such as lions and Amur leopards, and a wide variety of birds.

5. Huntington Beach State Park

This preserve in Murrells Inlet, a pristine beach and coastal area, attracts many birds, making it one of the best birding areas on the East Coast. It also offers excellent surf fishing, camping, nature programs, and an annual arts festival.

SOUTH CAROLINA

6. Middleton Place Plantation

The House Museum at this National Historic Landmark was built in 1755. There is something blooming year-round in the oldest landscaped gardens in North America. Stableyards allow visitors to imagine life on a Colonial plantation.

7. Patriots Point Naval and Maritime Museum

Located in Mount Pleasant, the museum's centerpiece is the USS *Yorktown*, an aircraft carrier built during World War II that served until 1970. Patriots Point also hosts a fleet of National Historic Landmark ships, a Cold War Memorial, and the only Vietnam Support Base Camp in the United States.

8. Riverbanks Zoo and Garden

This zoo in Columbia attracts more than a million yearly visitors to see lions, tigers, primates, and thousands of other animals in a botanical garden setting, including natural habitat exhibits, scenic river views, and historic landmarks.

9. South Carolina Aquarium

Tour sixty South Carolina habitats, from the mountains to the sea, and see creatures from around the world without leaving this facility in Charleston. Among the highlights is the state's only hospital for sick and injured sea turtles.

10. South Carolina State Museum

This is the biggest museum in the southeastern United States. It is located in Columbia in a former cloth mill that opened in 1894 and was the world's first totally electric textile mill. The museum tells the story of South Carolina's history through art, history, science, and technology.

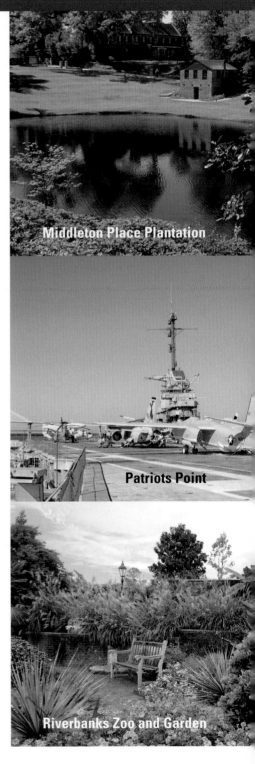

Middleton Place Plantation

Patriots Point

Riverbanks Zoo and Garden

The Arthur Ravenel Jr. Bridge across the Cooper River is 2.5 miles (4 km) long, making it the longest cable-stayed bridge in the Western Hemisphere. Completed in 2005, it was built to allow large ships to pass beneath it and to withstand hurricane-force winds.

Carolina down to the St. Johns River in north Florida. The barrier islands are separated from the mainland by saltwater marshes and estuaries. Hilton Head Island, near the southern tip of the state, is the best known of these islands and is a popular vacation spot.

Waterways

Thousands of years ago, the Atlantic Coastal Plain in South Carolina was covered with water. As the waters gradually receded, swamps, marshes, and small lakes remained. The state's largest lakes are artificial. The biggest lake in South Carolina is Lake Marion. It was created by a dam built on the Santee River in the early 1940s. Lake Marion has an area of 173 square miles (448 sq km) and covers parts of five counties.

South Carolina is drained by three major river systems that empty into the Atlantic Ocean. They are the Santee, the Savannah, and the Pee Dee. Around the middle of the state is the Santee, which flows southeast into the Atlantic Ocean after 143 miles (230 km). The Santee and its tributaries are South Carolina's most important river system. To the south along the border with Georgia is the Savannah River. It stretches 314 miles (505 km) to the ocean near Savannah, Georgia. In the north is the Pee Dee, which empties into Winyah Bay near Georgetown. For years, South Carolinians have used the power of all this flowing water to produce usable energy called hydroelectric power.

Climate

Overall, South Carolina has a humid, subtropical climate, with hot, generally humid summers, and mild winters. Humidity refers to the amount of moisture in the air. High humidity can make hot temperatures feel even hotter. The Atlantic Coast is the warmest part of the state, and the high elevations of the mountains in the northwest are the coldest. Average January temperatures in Charleston range from around 38 degrees Fahrenheit (3 degrees Celsius) to 60°F (16°C), while they range

Hurricane Hugo caused heavy damage in South Carolina in 1989.

from around 30°F (–1°C) to 50°F (10°C) in the Blue Ridge Mountains. These mountains are often covered with snow, but winters in the rest of South Carolina are generally mild. In most of the state, it is unusual to get more than a dusting of snow.

During the summer, temperatures in the low country may even soar above 100°F (38°C). Ocean breezes and cool water along the coast help to make the heat more tolerable. Rainfall in the state is considerable. In the Blue Ridge Mountains, more than 70 inches (178 centimeters) of rain fall each year. The entire state's average rainfall is about 50 inches (127 cm).

South Carolina residents seldom have to deal with heavy snowstorms, but tropical storms hit the state from time to time. One of the worst was the Sea Islands hurricane of August 1893. More than one thousand people were killed, mostly by drowning, in Georgia and South Carolina. Some thirty thousand people were left homeless. More recently, in September 1989, Hurricane Hugo destroyed homes, knocked down trees, and caused billions of dollars in damage in the Sea Islands and elsewhere in the low country. The storm killed thirty-five people in South Carolina. A storm went past South Carolina in early October of 2015, but it caused a one thousand-year rainfall. This means there is only a one in one thousand chance of this much rain falling in any year. On October 4,

Charleston received a one-day record of 24 inches (61 cm) of rain. The worst flooding ever in South Carolina killed at least six people, and there were two hundred water rescues over one weekend.

Wildlife

About two-thirds of the land in South Carolina is still made up of woods. There are four state forests and four national forest areas, and there is forestland in the forty-seven state parks. On the coastal plain, there are oak, red maple, hickory, and cypress trees, and palmetto trees are a familiar sight near the shore. Oak and hemlock trees grow in the Blue Ridge Mountains. Hickories, oaks, and dogwoods can be found in the Piedmont. Forests of cypress, sweet gum, and other trees grow in wet areas. Pine trees of many varieties can be found all over South Carolina.

A wide variety of native plants grow wild in South Carolina and, in many cases, also grow in gardens. The mountainous areas are especially known for their colorful azaleas, rhododendrons, and mountain laurel. Swamps and river bottoms feature plants such as honeysuckle, Venus flytrap, and yellow jessamine, the widely grown state flower.

In addition to the state flower, South Carolina also has an official state wildflower: the goldenrod. This widespread wildflower has tall stems with showy yellow flowers that create lovely fields of gold. Although often maligned as causing allergies, goldenrod is almost never the cause of hay fever symptoms. More likely the cause is ragweed, which blooms at around the same time as goldenrod. Ragweed pollen is light and spread by the wind, so it can easily affect people. Goldenrod pollen, on the other hand, is heavy and sticky, and usually not blown around by the wind. Bees and other insects pollinate goldenrod, which is relished for its abundant nectar.

South Carolina's forests and hills are home to many animals. Herds of white-tailed deer, the state animal, range freely through the countryside. South Carolina also has bears, bobcats, opossums,

Black bears are common in some parts of the state.

A poisonous water moccasin seeks prey in the Francis Beidler Forest.

raccoons, squirrels, foxes, and cottontail rabbits. Birds such as wrens, orioles, catbirds, hawks, and eagles fly through South Carolina skies and nest in the trees and thickets.

Waterfowl such as ducks, geese, and swans swim across the state's lakes and ponds. Egrets and herons live in the swamps. Trout, carp, catfish, and striped bass, the state fish, are common freshwater fish. In the coastal waters are sharks, dolphins, giant turtles, and an occasional sperm whale, as well as oysters, crabs, and clams. The swamps and marshes have alligators and many species of frogs and snakes, including poisonous water moccasins and copperheads.

Pollution, overhunting or overfishing, and loss of habitat have harmed some types of animals. Dozens of South Carolina's animal and plant species are listed as threatened or endangered. Among the endangered animals are hawksbill, Kemp's ridley, and leatherback sea turtles, the red-cockaded woodpecker, and a mussel called the Carolina heelsplitter. Laws limit or prohibit hunting or fishing for certain species, and breeding programs have been set up to increase certain animal populations.

State Spider

The Carolina Wolf Spider is South Carolina's official arachnid. A female's body can be almost an inch [2.5 cm] long, and with the legs included, the spider is huge. They live on the ground or in burrows, and they eat insects that they catch by pouncing. They rarely bite, and they aren't dangerous to humans, preferring to run away.

10 KEY PLANTS AND ANIMALS

American Alligator

Eastern Tiger Swallowtail Butterfly

Flowering Dogwood

1. American Alligator

Alligators live in the swamps and waters of the coastal plain. They often bask in the sun, and they can live for more than sixty years. They are listed as a threatened species, partly because of habitat loss and pollution.

2. American Oystercatcher

One of two species of oystercatcher that breeds in North America, this shorebird finds plenty of great habitat in South Carolina's abundant beaches, marshes, mudflats, and salt marshes. It eats snails, sea worms, and aquatic insects, in addition to shellfish.

3. Bobwhite Quail

The "gamebird of the South" is named for its distinctive cry, which sounds like "bob-WHITE." They are found throughout South Carolina, but they are particularly abundant in the coastal plain area. Adults eat seeds, but babies eat mostly insects.

4. Eastern Tiger Swallowtail Butterfly

South Carolina's official butterfly is the Eastern tiger swallowtail. The adult male has yellow and black wings. The female's wings can be either yellow or bluish-black. These butterflies use long, tubelike tongues to feed on flower nectar.

5. Flowering Dogwood

This tree, which is native to South Carolina, reaches a height of 20 to 30 feet (6 to 9.1 m). It sends out snowy-white flowers before leaves.

6. Kudzu

Sometimes called "The Vine That Ate the South," kudzu was imported from Japan in the 1870s. It can grow as fast as 1 foot (30 cm) a day, wrapping around almost anything else in its path. This vine is considered a weed.

Kudzu

7. Spotted Salamander

This amphibian is known for its dark-colored body dotted with bright spots of color. Spotted salamanders spend much of their lives underground in the woods. When they are threatened, their skin releases a white, sticky liquid that poisons attackers.

Spotted Salamander

8. Striped Bass

This is the state fish of South Carolina. It has a silvery body and stripes running from gills to tail. Sport fishers prize the size and fighting spirit of the striped bass, which can weigh 30 to 40 pounds (14 to 18 kg).

9. Wild Hog

These descendants of escaped Spanish pigs live in all forty-six South Carolina counties. They are not native to the area and can be destructive to native plants and ecosystems. Wild hogs are often hunted, sometimes using teams of dogs.

Striped Bass

10. Wild Turkey

These magnificent birds are found year-round almost everywhere in South Carolina, but they are most common in some regions of the Piedmont. They travel in flocks and use strong feet to search for snails, nuts, insects and berries.

The Santa Elena Festival, as painted by John Berkey, was brought to South Carolina by the state's first European settlers.

From the Beginning

Archaeologists digging near the Savannah River, in an area now part of South Carolina, have found evidence that people may have been living in the region as far back as sixteen thousand years ago or more, during the last Ice Age. These tribes hunted, fished, and gathered nuts and berries. Stone spear points that they made can still be found in the hills of South Carolina. Pieces of Native American pottery can be found today in parts of the state.

By the sixteenth century, tribes of Cherokee were living in the northwestern part of present-day South Carolina. Other groups living in the area included the Edistoes, Waterees, and Keowees. By the end of the seventeenth century, the Yamasee and Catawba tribes had also settled there.

Fifteen thousand to thirty thousand Native Americans may have been living in the region when European explorers arrived in the sixteenth century. The Native Americans lacked **immunity** to the diseases carried by the Europeans. As a result, many thousands died from diseases such as smallpox, influenza, and measles. Others died in battle or were taken as slaves. The Native American population was greatly reduced, and its way of life was never the same.

Settlers flee Native American warriors at the start of the Yamasee War.

The European Settlers

South Carolina eventually became an English colony, but only after both the French and the Spanish had attempted to start permanent settlements there. In 1521, a Spanish ship from the colony of Santo Domingo in the Caribbean landed in Winyah Bay on the coast of present-day South Carolina. The Spaniards invited some Native Americans onto their ship. Once they were aboard, however, they were made prisoners. The Spanish then set sail for Santo Domingo, taking the Native Americans as slaves. One of the Native Americans became a servant to Lucas Vásquez de Ayllón, who had helped pay for the expedition. The servant told wonderful stories about his homeland, which he claimed was a rich land ruled by a giant king.

In the summer of 1526, Ayllón set out for the Carolina coast with about five hundred Spaniards and some black slaves—the first of hundreds of thousands to be brought to the American South. He started a settlement named San Miguel de Gualdape. It was the first European settlement on land that is now part of the United States. But the Spaniards soon discovered that the wonderful stories of wealth and treasure were untrue, and many Spanish settlers died from hunger and disease. After Ayllón's death, the slaves rebelled against their captors. That winter, surviving settlers tried to return to Europe, though many died during the difficult journey home.

In 1562, a group of Protestants from France set up a small settlement near what is now Port Royal. They had suffered religious discrimination in France, where most people and the country's rulers were Catholic. The French Protestants wanted to live where they could freely practice their religion. This settlement also failed. As they encountered hardships and their food and supplies ran out, the colonists tried to sail back to France. Many starved to death on the way.

In 1566, Spain established a settlement called Santa Elena on Port Royal Sound, near present-day Beaufort. It had more than four hundred people residing in it by 1575. For a short time, it served as the capital of Spain's La Florida province, which included a large area of the southeastern part of North America.

In 1587, as a result of English attacks on Spanish Florida, Santa Elena was abandoned, and by the early 1600s,

The First and Last Shot

Confederate Edmund Ruffin is often credited as firing the first official shot of the American Civil War. On April 12, 1861 at 4:30 a.m., he is said to have fired a mortar round at Fort Sumter, held by Union forces. He symbolically fired a final shot in his own war when, hearing that the South had surrendered, he shot himself rather than submit to Northern rule.

England had taken possession of much of the land that is now South Carolina. In 1629, England's King Charles I gave a large tract of land—including present-day North Carolina and South Carolina—as a gift to Sir Robert Heath. He wanted it to be called Carolana, which is Latin for "land of Charles." (Later, the spelling was changed to Carolina.) Sir Robert did very little to attract settlers, and in 1663, King Charles II, son of Charles I, gave the colony to eight noblemen called lords proprietors. They offered land, freedom of religion, and a new way of life to anyone who would travel there.

In 1670, two shiploads of people landed in the region. Many were from the island of Barbados in the Caribbean, which was then under English rule. They started a settlement at Albemarle Point, later moving it a short distance away to Oyster Point. The settlement was known as Charles Towne (present-day Charleston). As it grew, more settlers moved into other parts of the area. Early in the next century, Carolina was divided into North Carolina and South Carolina.

Native Americans in South Carolina often cooperated with the newcomers, but the colonists took more and more land for rice and indigo fields. These were important crops before the arrival of cotton. English traders also often abused the Native Americans and took many as slaves. The anger of the Yamasee and other tribes increased. In 1715, their warriors began an attack up along the coast of South Carolina, burning homes and killing settlers as they went. It was the start of the Yamasee War. Many settlers fled to Charles

The Native People

Native Americans had lived in the region now known as South Carolina for thousands of years before European settlers arrived. When the Europeans (first Spanish, later French, and finally English) arrived, there were twenty-nine nations, or distinct tribes, residing in the area. They were divided into different language groups. The tribes that lived in the low country and near the coast spoke variations of the Algonquian language. Groups that spoke the Siouan and Iroquoian languages lived in the up-country and Piedmont areas.

The tribes had developed sophisticated civilizations. When Europeans arrived, there was a lot of trade among the cultures. Many tribes were known for their expert pottery techniques, and art, tools, and other items were exchanged among tribes. Some people would learn multiple languages so they could communicate with neighboring tribes that spoke another language. The tribes practiced agriculture, growing crops such as beans, squash, and corn. All tribes primarily used the bow and arrow to hunt game such as deer and turkeys. Along the coast they caught fish and harvested shellfish. All tribes used dugout canoes made from hollowed-out logs to move along the region's many rivers.

Contact with Europeans exposed the Native Americans to many new diseases. Their bodies did not have any natural immunity to these illnesses so many thousands died of such things as smallpox and measles. Settlers traded with

Members of the Cherokee and Catawba tribes gather at a powwow.

the Native Americans, but they also took some Native Americans as slaves. Settlers used the money they got from selling Native American slaves to purchase African slaves. The Yamasee and the Tuscarora rose up against the settlers in the Yamasee War (1715–1717) but were defeated and mostly fled the area.

Though many of the original Native American nations of South Carolina are extinct, have moved to other areas, or were absorbed into other Native American groups, several tribes remain. These include the Catawba, Cherokee, Chicora, Chicora-Waccamaw, Edisto, Pee Dee, Santee, and Yamasee. Some live on reservations, while others live in the community. The Catawba Indian Nation is the only federally recognized tribe in the state.

Spotlight on the Catawba

Catawba is pronounced "cuh-TAW-buh." It comes from the word *katapu*, which means "fork in the river." The Catawba usually call themselves Ye Iswa, which means "people of the river."

Distribution: The Catawba originally lived in both South and North Carolina, but today they mostly live in South Carolina. Some were forcibly relocated to Oklahoma. Now, many members of the tribe live on their reservation. A tribal council provides government inside the reservation.

Language: The Catawba language is almost lost. Today, no members of the tribe speak it well, though some know a few words and a few are trying to revive it. Most Catawba today speak English.

Homes: The Catawba lived in villages with nearby farmland. They made houses with wooden frames and walls of tree bark. Ceremonies and meetings were held in a large round building.

Clothing and Decoration: Women wore skirts that wrapped round their waists. They also wore a top that left their right shoulder bare. Men wore breechcloths made from soft deerskin. Both men and women wore moccasins. Hair was usually kept long. Women wore it in a bun at the back of their heads, while men wore a topknot. They sometimes decorated their skin with tattoos or painted their bodies before ceremonies or battles.

Food: Catawba women did most of the farming. They grew maize (corn), squash, and beans. The men did most of the hunting, and they also went fishing and harvested.

Blackbeard and his crew terrorized merchant ships off the coast of the Carolinas.

Towne, but before long, the Yamasee and their allies were defeated. Another threat to the colonists was the pirates who sailed the coast. They docked their ships at ports and raided the cities. Among these pirates was Edward Teach, better known as Blackbeard.

In addition to these dangers, the English settlers in South Carolina also feared that Spain or France would try to take over the territory. Partly because the lords proprietors refused to provide money for the colony's defense, the settlers rebelled against them and asked King George I for help. He eventually took control of the colony, and it was ruled directly by the British monarch through an appointed royal governor.

Revolution and Statehood

By the mid–1700s, many people in South Carolina and other colonies were unhappy with the British government. Britain wanted profit from its colonies, and it also wanted them to pay for the military support it provided. So Britain taxed the colonists heavily, adding to the costs of such things as paper, ink, and tea. However, no colonists were members of Parliament, the governing body of Britain that decided to impose the taxation. The colonists wanted to change Britain's tax and trade rules and to have more of a voice in government. In September 1774, leaders from South Carolina and other American colonies met in Philadelphia for the First Continental Congress. They decided not to allow any goods to be imported from Britain and sent a list of grievances to the British king, George III. These grievances were ignored.

By April 1775, colonists in New England were fighting against the British Army—in effect, the American Revolution had begun. South Carolina was the first colony to declare its independence, in March 1776. In July 1776, representatives from all thirteen colonies voted to declare independence. Supporters of independence were called **Patriots**. Other colonists, known as **Loyalists**, sided with the British.

A small British force had already bombarded the harbor of Charles Towne, but it was beaten back at Sullivan's Island in June 1776. This denied the British an early foothold in the South. South Carolina got its state tree and the image on its flag from the Sabal palmetto trees that were used to hastily fortify the walls of Sullivan's Island. The trees were so soft and spongy that cannon balls either bounced off harmlessly or just sank into the wood without destroying the wall. Two years later, the British began an assault on the South. They gained control of Georgia, and in May 1780, they captured Charles Towne. A few months later, British troops crushed Patriot forces and units of the colonists' Continental Army at the Battle of Camden.

However, the Patriots never gave up. Well over one hundred battles were fought in South Carolina—more than in any other state. Forces under General Nathanael Greene and Patriot leader Francis Marion harassed and defeated British troops and their allies all over the region. At the Battle of Kings Mountain in 1780, some nine hundred Patriot frontiersmen from the Blue Ridge Mountains banded together. In about one hour, they

A band of one thousand frontiersmen decisively defeated Tory soldiers, made up mostly of South Carolina Loyalists, in the Battle of King's Mountain in 1780.

Making a Sabal Palmetto

The Sabal palmetto is South Carolina's state tree. It earned that title not just because it is common in coastal regions of the state, but also because Sabal palmetto trunks were used to fortify Fort Moultrie during the Revolutionary War. British cannonballs bounced off the soft trunks. You can make a replica of the state's most notable tree.

What You Need

A cardboard paper towel roll

A brown paper bag (lunch bag size)

Six to eight pieces of green construction paper

Glue

A rubber band or clothes pins

What To Do

- Cut the bottom out of the brown paper bag. Slip the bag over the paper towel roll. Gather the bag together at the base and glue the bag to the paper towel roll. Either let the glue dry or use clothespins or a rubber band to hold the bag at the base until the glue is dry.

- Push the bag down from the top, crinkling the paper. Apply several lines of glue to the paper towel roll. Pull the bag up and press the paper bag onto the roll. Make sure the paper wrinkles and twists to create a texture similar to a palm tree's trunk. Glue the top, trimming or tucking in any excess.

- Fold a piece of green construction paper in half (the short way) and cut from the corner of the folded end in an arc shape to the corner of the opposite folded end. The cut should resemble the curve of a rainbow. Cut two or three small triangles in the curved edge of the paper. Then fold the paper like a fan. Open the paper, and it should resemble the leaf of a Sabal palmetto. Repeat until you have enough leaves, and glue them to the top of the paper towel roll.

defeated a regiment of more than one thousand Loyalist soldiers. The tide of the war in the southern colonies turned in favor of the Patriots at Cowpens in January 1781. General Daniel Morgan's soldiers routed a unit of top British troops.

The main British army in the South retreated to Virginia, then surrendered after a crushing defeat at Yorktown, Virginia, in October 1781. With the signing of a peace treaty two years later, officially ending the war, the colonies were free of British rule. On May 23, 1788, South Carolina ratified the new US Constitution and became the eighth state of the Union (another term for the United States).

Slavery and the Road to the Civil War

From South Carolina's earliest days as a colony, farmers used slaves to work in the fields. Most were black people brought to the American mainland either directly from Africa or via the islands in the Caribbean. As demand for export crops such as rice and indigo increased, more and more black slaves were brought to South Carolina. By the early 1700s, slaves outnumbered white people.

In 1793, the cotton gin was invented, providing an easier way to remove the seeds from cotton. Soon after, machines were developed to manufacture cloth on a large scale. Cotton was now in heavy demand and became South Carolina's biggest cash crop and export. Cotton plantations grew and prospered, built on slave labor. Because of the large slave population, the colony's plantation owners, or planters, were always afraid of a major revolt. By the early 1800s, they also began to fear that the federal government could act to abolish (end) **slavery**.

Many South Carolinians were also concerned about tariffs, which are taxes on products traded between countries. In 1828, the federal government imposed high tariffs on manufactured goods imported from abroad. (A tariff helps protect a country's own products by making imports more expensive to buy.) The 1828 tariff helped industrial states in the North, but it did not help South Carolina, which mostly produced crops like

Deadly Earthquake

Though South Carolina mostly worries about hurricanes, earthquakes are another natural disaster that threatens the state. South Carolina has an average of ten to fifteen earthquakes each year, most relatively minor and below magnitude 3. However, a 7.3 magnitude quake struck Charleston in 1886, killing sixty people. It was the most powerful quake to ever hit the eastern United States.

cotton. In fact, it meant that planters in the South had to pay much higher prices for manufactured goods.

South Carolina's leaders called a state convention and declared that the federal laws establishing the tariff of 1828, and a later one in 1832, violated the rights of states under the US Constitution. They claimed that a state had the right to declare any such federal law null and void. (This asserted right became known as the principle of "nullification.") They threatened that South Carolina would secede from the Union if the federal government tried to collect these tariffs in their state.

President Andrew Jackson got Congress to pass a measure allowing him to use the army and navy, if necessary, to enforce federal law in South Carolina. He also worked out a compromise that reduced the tariffs. South Carolina's leaders agreed, and the threat of secession was removed for a while.

However, South Carolina's leaders believed that the future of slavery would be in danger if Abraham Lincoln was elected president. In December 1860, a month after

Magnolia Plantation on the Ashley River was built in 1697, making it one of the South's oldest plantations.

This 1862 photo shows slaves preparing cotton for the gin on Smith's Plantation on Port Royal Island.

Lincoln was elected, South Carolina seceded from the United States. Over the next several months, ten other Southern states also seceded, and all eleven joined together to form the Confederate States of America. President Lincoln did not accept the right of states to secede from the Union. He was determined to keep the Union from breaking up.

The Civil War

The Civil War began in earnest in April 1861, when the Union commander refused to surrender Fort Sumter in the harbor of Charleston. The Confederates fired upon the fort for more than thirty hours, inflicting heavy damage, until the Union forces finally gave up. No soldier on either side was killed during the bombardment. Meanwhile, Lincoln called for volunteers to fight against the rebellion and ordered the navy to **blockade** Southern ports.

To protect the harbor, South Carolinians built a series of forts equipped with heavy guns. They also put mines and torpedo boats in the water. These defenses protected Charleston for most of the war.

In May 1862, a black sailor named Robert Smalls was able to pilot a Confederate steamer out of the harbor and give it to the Union fleet, which was blocking the coast and keeping supplies away. The information he gave Union officers about Charleston's defenses helped them launch an attack, but the attack failed.

10 ★ KEY CITIES ★ ★ ★

1. Columbia: population 129,272

Named after Christopher Columbus, the state's largest city serves as its capital. It is home to many cultural attractions and hosts many festivals. It is located in Richmond and Lexington Counties.

2. Charleston: population 120,083

Located where the Cooper and Ashley Rivers meet the Atlantic Ocean, Charleston is South Carolina's oldest city. It was named after England's King Charles II. For several years in a row, Charleston was designated one of the country's most friendly cities.

3. North Charleston: population 97,471

North Charleston was incorporated in 1972 as the ninth-largest city in the state. It has since become the third-largest city. It is a leader in industry, and the state's top producer in retail sales. The Detyens Shipyards is located there.

4. Mount Pleasant: population 67,843

This suburban town is home to Patriots Point, a museum where several Navy ships are displayed. There are many historical buildings in its Old Village neighborhood.

5. Rock Hill: population 66,154

York County's largest city is located midway between Columbia, South Carolina, and Charlotte, North Carolina. A famous Rock Hill landmark are the four 22-foot (6.7 m) bronze statues called the Civitas, which represent the four different industries in the city. The city was severely damaged by Hurricane Hugo in 1989.

Columbia

Rock Hill

★ SOUTH CAROLINA ★

6. Greenville: population 58,409

Greenville, the fastest growing city in South Carolina, is known for its strong job market. It attracts many young professionals with its active local theaters and many major concerts. Lovely parks and waterfalls draw tourists.

7. Summerville: population 43,392

Located mostly in Dorchester County, Summerville was settled shortly after the Revolutionary War as a place to escape Charleston's mosquitoes. The city is known for its pine trees.

8. Sumter: population 40,524

This city is located in Sumter County in the east central Piedmont region. It was named after General Thomas Sumter, a hero of the Revolutionary War known as the "Fighting Gamecock." Shaw Air Force Base provides employment for many residents.

Shaw Air Force Base, Sumter

9. Hilton Head Island: population 37,099

This resort island town is a very popular tourist destination, attracting millions of visitors each year. The population can grow to 275,000 during the summer season. Despite the crowds, the city works to protect its natural beauty, preserving trees and regulating development.

10. Florence: population 37,056

Located in the Pee Dee region of northeast South Carolina, Florence is a major railroad hub and a center of business and industry. It has a downtown historic district with many preserved buildings, and the entire downtown area is in the midst of revitalization as of the publication of this book.

Florence National Cemetery

The Civil War began with the firing on Fort Sumter.

In July 1863, Union forces launched an attack on Fort Wagner, which protected Charleston Harbor. The attack was spearheaded by the Fifty-Fourth Massachusetts Regiment, made up of black men. Most came from the North, but one-quarter of them came from the South and the Caribbean. The 1989 Academy Award-winning movie *Glory* told the story of this unsuccessful Union attack. It wasn't until mid-February 1865, six weeks from the end of the war, that Union troops were able to capture a badly battered Charleston.

In early 1865, Union troops, under the command of General William T. Sherman, burned the city of Columbia and cut a wide path of destruction as they marched through the state. The largest Confederate army, located in Virginia, surrendered to Union forces on April 9, 1865. Fighting ended everywhere over the following weeks. After four years of bloody fighting, the South was defeated, and the Civil War was over.

Recovering from the War

For South Carolina, the Civil War changed everything. The Emancipation Proclamation, signed by President Lincoln on January 1, 1863, essentially freed all slaves in the state (some four hundred thousand as of the 1860 US census). Those who had not already escaped were freed as territory fell into Union hands. At the end of 1865, the Thirteenth

Amendment to the US Constitution abolished slavery throughout the United States.

More than twenty thousand South Carolina soldiers died during the war. The economy was ruined, and resources were few. The state had a long, hard road of rebuilding ahead.

Right after the war, white leaders who did not want the South to change governed South Carolina. They passed laws that restricted the rights of former slaves and forced them, in effect, to continue working on plantations. By 1867, however, the federal government had taken a more active role in managing the states that had formed the Confederacy.

During what became known as the period of Reconstruction, the US Congress appointed military commanders to take control. The federal government required

Swamp Fever

The mosquito-filled areas of the low country were plagued by what people at the time called swamp fever. We now know that they suffered from several different mosquito-borne diseases, including malaria and yellow fever. The diseases killed thousands. Today there is a vaccine for yellow fever, and mosquito control has wiped out both diseases in the United States.

Slaves provided the labor in the cotton fields of South Carolina before the Civil War.

South Carolina's official state craft is sweetgrass basket weaving. African slaves were able to keep up their ancestral basket weaving practices after they were stolen from their homes and enslaved in South Carolina. The tradition has been passed down through many generations. Baskets made today are still very much like baskets woven in the parts of Africa where their ancestors lived.

Southern states to pass new constitutions that kept former Confederate leaders from governing and gave former slaves the right to vote.

On June 25, 1868, South Carolina was readmitted to the Union. Under Reconstruction, African Americans began to gain rights as free Americans. Some were even elected to public office. Many black children were able to attend school for the first time.

These measures angered many white people. Some of them resorted to violence. Some whites joined a secret society known as the Ku Klux Klan. Dressed in white robes or sheets, they burned crosses to frighten those who opposed them. They attacked both black and white public officials to drive them out of the new government. They used violence to intimidate and prevent black residents from voting. In what was known as lynching, black people who angered white people or were considered guilty of a crime might be carried off and executed, often by hanging.

In April 1877, federal troops were removed from South Carolina. Wade Hampton, a wealthy plantation owner, became governor, and Reconstruction ended. African Americans soon began to lose the rights they had won, especially after Benjamin Tillman became governor in 1890. Tillman promoted programs to help poor farmers, but he also believed in "white supremacy." He got the state constitution rewritten to limit voting rights for African Americans and require that black students attend separate schools from those attended by white children.

So-called Jim Crow laws were also passed to require segregation—separation of whites and blacks—on trains and buses, in restaurants, and in other public facilities. These laws remained in effect until Congress passed the Civil Rights Act of 1964, which outlawed discrimination in public places and in the workplace.

In another way, South Carolina did make a recovery from the effects of the Civil War. In time, the state's economy began to improve. The ports hummed with activity. Farmers

Marines have trained on Parris Island since 1915.

were able to sell their crops. Cotton textile mills, which were highly profitable, provided many jobs.

Not everyone profited, however. Work in the mills was mainly for white people. Families often had trouble making ends meet, and young children were sent to work in mills and factories. The hours were long, the pay was low, and workers, especially children, were often injured on the job or became ill as a result of poor working conditions. Labor laws establishing a minimum work age and improving some working conditions were eventually passed in the late 1930s.

Ups and Downs

When the Great Depression hit the United States in the 1930s, many South Carolinians lost their jobs and homes. The prices farmers received for their crops fell sharply. Many people left the state in search of better opportunities. African Americans, who had already been suffering from discrimination and a lack of opportunities, were especially hard hit. Increasing numbers of black people moved to northern cities, including New York City, Chicago, and Detroit.

World War II (1939–1945) also helped the economy. South Carolina workers went back to the factories and farms to provide the supplies needed on the battlefront. Military bases opened near Charleston, providing other jobs. After the United States entered the war in 1941, many South Carolinians served in the armed forces. The Marine Corps Recruit Depot on Parris Island opened in 1915 and thrived after the end of World War I. There was a drop in the recruitment of marines during the Great Depression, and that

Coretta Scott King (in sunglasses) joins striking hospital workers in Charleston in 1969.

affected the base. However, when World War II began in 1939, recruits flocked to the base, which received new barracks and a training facility. Today, male recruits from the Eastern United States and all female marine recruits train at Parris Island.

During the twentieth century, South Carolina reduced its reliance on a few big crops and developed tourism and other industries to help the economy grow. The economy suffered again in the recession, or economic downturn, that hit both the nation and the world starting in late 2007. By 2015, even though the state's unemployment rate was higher than the nation's rate, there were more people with jobs in South Carolina than ever before.

During the 1950s and 1960s, for the first time since the end of Reconstruction, the state's African Americans began to see progress. In the early 1950s, a state poll tax that prevented many black people from voting was eliminated. Measures were also taken to curb the Ku Klux Klan, which had revived in the 1920s.

Many white people in South Carolina remained opposed to ending segregation in schools. South Carolina's Strom Thurmond ran for president in 1948 as a "states' rights" candidate opposed to ending segregation. He easily won the vote in South Carolina. He later became a US senator, representing the state for almost fifty years. But more and more white South Carolinians started listening to civil rights leaders such as Dr. Martin Luther King Jr., Isaiah DeQuincey Newman, Benjamin Mays, and Jesse Jackson.

Changing Times

South Carolina's first chapters of the National Association for the Advancement of Colored People (NAACP) had been set up in 1917. With the civil rights movement gaining momentum in the 1950s, the NAACP attracted more members and became a stronger political voice. Sit-ins, marches, and demonstrations were organized to oppose segregation and discrimination against African Americans. The South Carolina tune "We Shall Overcome" became the movement's anthem. The many black people who had before been voiceless now held the power to seek justice.

The 1954 Supreme Court decision barring segregation in public education met with resistance in the state. However, by the end of the 1960s, the state's public schools were all integrated. Black students and white students no longer had to attend separate schools.

Racial tensions did not go away. In 1962, the legislature voted to fly the Confederate flag from the top of the State House in Columbia. The flag had different meanings for different people. For many African Americans and others, it stood for a long history of enslavement and oppression of black people. The NAACP protested and started a boycott of the state's tourism industry. The National Collegiate Athletic Association decided not to play any championship events in the state. Many companies dropped plans to hold

People sing "We Shall Overcome" at the College of Charleston TD Arena during a June 19, 2015, prayer vigil for the nine victims of the Emanuel AME Church shootings.

The South Carolina Highway Patrol Honor Guard removes the Confederate battle flag from the State House grounds on July 10, 2015.

conventions in the state. In 2000, the legislature did vote to remove the flag from the Capitol Dome but agreed to place a smaller version of the flag on State House grounds next to a monument to fallen Confederate soldiers.

In a sign of progress, Nikki Haley, a South Carolina state legislator and the daughter of immigrants from India, was elected governor in 2010. She became the first member of a racial minority, and the first woman, to serve as the state's chief executive.

A critical moment in state history occurred in the summer of 2015 when a young man who believed in white supremacy shot nine African Americans at a Bible study in Charleston's Emanuel African Methodist Episcopal Church. Among the dead was a state senator, Reverend Clementa Pinckney. President Barack Obama attended the funeral for those murdered and delivered the eulogy. The families of the slain people forgave the killer, and whites and blacks joined to share their grief over the killings and to pray for the victims. In a true sign of progress, there was no violence during any of the protests or the prayer vigils.

A short time later, Governor Haley asked the legislature to vote to remove the Confederate battle flag from the State House grounds. She signed the bill that authorized its removal on July 9, 2015. It came down the next morning in front of cheering crowds.

10 KEY DATES IN STATE HISTORY

1. 1526

Lucas Vásquez de Ayllón founds San Miguel de Gualdape, the first European settlement on what is now US soil.

2. April 1670

English settlers establish the first permanent European settlement in what is now South Carolina. After being moved nearby, it grows into the city of Charleston.

3. June 28, 1776

Early in the American Revolution, British forces attack what became Charleston and are beaten back at Sullivan's Island.

4. December 20, 1860

South Carolina becomes the first state to secede from the Union; it is readmitted in 1868.

5. April 12, 1861

Confederate troops fire artillery on Fort Sumter, starting the Civil War. No casualties were reported in thirty-four hours of bombardment.

6. September 1963

African Americans are admitted to previously all-white public schools in South Carolina.

7. September 21, 1989

Hurricane Hugo, which makes landfall at midnight, causes billions of dollars in damage in South Carolina. Wind gusts in Charleston reach 108 miles per hour (174 km/h).

8. August 1995

The Citadel military academy in Charleston admits its first female student.

9. November 2, 2010

Nikki Haley, the daughter of immigrants from Punjab, India, becomes the first member of a racial minority, and the first woman, to be elected governor of South Carolina.

10. June 18, 2015

Nine African Americans are shot and killed during a Bible study at Emanuel African Methodist Episcopal Church in Charleston.

The Carolina shag was so popular that it was named the State Dance in South Carolina in 1984.

The People

South Carolina has a smaller proportion of foreign-born residents than most other states. In all, about 96 percent of the state's residents today were born in the United States. Further, a very low percentage of native-born South Carolina residents permanently move out of their home state. In fact, three out of every four people who live in South Carolina were born there. Many claim that their ancestors were among those who settled South Carolina centuries ago. Generations of South Carolina residents are proud of their families' long connection with their state.

In its early days, South Carolina was mostly rural. It was a state of big plantations and small family farms, and the economy was based on agriculture. Today, three out of five people in South Carolina live in urban, or city, areas. Columbia, the capital, is the biggest city. Other large, populous cities include Charleston, North Charleston, Rock Hill, Mount Pleasant, Greenville, Summerville, Spartanburg, and Sumter.

About two-thirds of South Carolina's people are white. Most of the rest are African American. There are small numbers of Native Americans, some of which are members of tribes that populated South Carolina before the arrival of European settlers. There is also a small percentage of Asian Americans in the state. Hispanics, or Latinos, make up about 4 percent of the total state population.

Original Inhabitants

Long before Europeans settled in the region, many Native American groups were hunting, fishing, and farming on the land. They had developed their own governments, social structures, and traditions. As European explorers and settlers arrived, the Native American population declined sharply. A great deal of this was due to diseases the Europeans brought with them, but many Native Americans also lost their lives in conflict or were captured as slaves and sent to the Caribbean or elsewhere.

The local Native American peoples also often lost their homelands. In 1830, President Andrew Jackson signed the Indian Removal Act. This act ordered many of the tribes that lived in the southeastern United States—including the Cherokee, Choctaw, Chickasaw, Muscogee, and Seminole—to leave their ancestral lands. They were forced to move to an area west of the Mississippi River designated as "Indian Territory." The Cherokee, who were then living in South Carolina and elsewhere in the southeast, were forced to march about 1,000 miles (1,600 km) to Oklahoma. Many died on the brutal journey, which is now called the **Trail of Tears**. Of the more than sixteen thousand Cherokee who were forced to make this terrible trip, between two thousand and six thousand died of starvation, cold, and disease. Once they arrived, they were in a hostile land that was completely unlike their homeland in the Carolinas.

Another tribe was pressured by the state into selling its land for new territory in North Carolina. This tribe, the Catawba, never received that land, but it did acquire a smaller reservation in South Carolina. In 1993, the tribe was awarded $50 million by the federal government in return for dropping its land claims. Today, there are a few thousand Catawba living in South Carolina. Many live near Rock Hill, close to their original territory along the banks of the Catawba River.

President Andrew Jackson signed the Indian Removal Act in 1830, which eventually put thousands of Cherokee on the Trail of Tears.

In all, there are about twelve thousand Native Americans in South Carolina. Many have tried to preserve their culture and share it with others. For example, the Day of the Catawba is an annual event held on the Saturday after Thanksgiving. It includes dance demonstrations, traditional music, and displays of Catawba pottery. Many of the languages that the First Peoples of South Carolina once spoke have been lost or are rarely spoken, but some elders are trying to keep the old languages alive, and some young people value and preserve their old culture.

Settlers from Europe

Wealthy English colonists from Barbados settled the city of Charleston (then known as Charles Towne) in 1670. They built large plantations and used slaves imported from Africa to work the land. They were joined by other settlers from the British Isles, including Irish from Northern Ireland and Scots-Irish and others from Scotland. Some of the early settlers were Protestants who did not belong to the Church of England. They were often discriminated against at home and so moved to the colonies in search of religious freedom.

In the colony's early days, Scottish immigrants were not allowed to hold office. Eventually, Scottish men and women went on to become governors, members of Congress, and state legislators. These days, Scottish cultural celebrations called ceilidhs (pronounced KAY-lays) are held in towns across South Carolina from Sumter to Aiken.

Most residents of South Carolina today are descendants of European settlers or are African Americans.

★ 10 ★ KEY PEOPLE ★ ★

James Brown

Stephen Colbert

Althea Gibson

1. James Mark Baldwin

Born in Columbia in 1861, James Mark Baldwin was a noted psychologist who helped spread this then-new field of study. He focused on developmental psychology and on how evolution related to the mind.

2. Mary McLeod Bethune

Born in 1875 in Mayesville to former slaves, Mary McLeod Bethune believed education was the key to success. She worked for the advancement of African Americans until her death in 1955.

3. James Brown

Known as the "Godfather of Soul" and recognized as one of the originators of funk music, James Brown was born in 1933 in Barnwell. He had sixteen hit singles on the R&B Billboard chart in a six-decade career.

4. Stephen Colbert

Comedian and TV personality Stephen Colbert was born in Washington, DC, but grew up on James Island in Charleston. He has hosted the *Colbert Report* and *The Late Show*, and was named one of the world's most influential people by *Time* magazine twice.

5. Althea Gibson

Althea Gibson, born in 1927 in Silver, was the first black woman to win Grand Slam tennis championships—she won eleven in the 1950s. In 1957, she was the first African American to be voted Female Athlete of the Year by the Associated Press.

SOUTH CAROLINA

6. Dizzy Gillespie

Dizzy (John Birks) Gillespie was a trumpet and trombone player born in 1917 in Cheraw. He revolutionized jazz with his fast-paced style called bebop. In 1975, he won a Grammy, and in 1989, he was awarded the National Medal of Arts.

7. Jesse Jackson

Jesse Jackson was born in Greenville during the depths of the Jim Crow segregation era. He grew up to become one of the country's most outspoken advocates for civil rights. This Baptist minister has twice sought the Democratic presidential nomination.

8. Francis Marion

Born in the colony of South Carolina around 1732, Francis Marion became a military hero in the American Revolution. He earned the nickname the Swamp Fox because he and his men often struck at night and then disappeared into the swamps.

9. Chris Rock

Chris Rock was born in Andrews, though his family later relocated to Brooklyn, New York. He is an actor, comedian, writer, and director who found fame on *Saturday Night Live*.

10. Thomas Sumter

Born in Virginia, Thomas Sumter moved to South Carolina in 1760 and made his name as a general in the American Revolution. Known as the Carolina Gamecock, he won several key battles in the state. He served in state and national legislatures and was a supporter of state's rights.

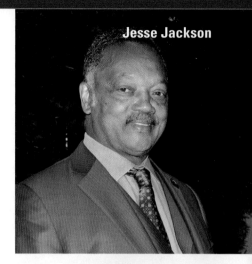

Jesse Jackson

Francis Marion

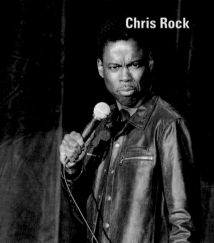

Chris Rock

Who South Carolinians Are

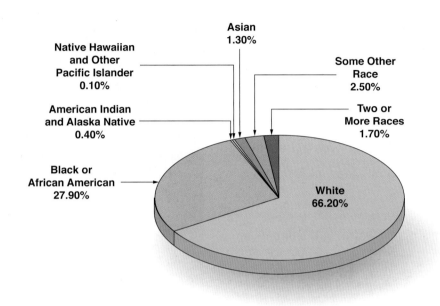

Asian
1.30%

Native Hawaiian
and Other
Pacific Islander
0.10%

Some Other
Race
2.50%

American Indian
and Alaska Native
0.40%

Two or
More Races
1.70%

Black or
African American
27.90%

White
66.20%

**Total Population
4,625,364**

Hispanic or Latino (of any race):
• 235,682 people (5.1%)

Note: The pie chart shows the
racial breakdown of the state's
population based on the categories
used by the US Bureau of the
Census. The Census Bureau
reports information for Hispanics
or Latinos separately, since they
may be of any race. Percentages
in the pie chart may not add to 100
because of rounding.

Source: US Bureau
of the Census, 2010 Census

Descendants of the early English, Scottish, and Irish settlers, and of immigrants from the British Isles who arrived and settled in this part of the country over the years, make up the largest single group of white people living in South Carolina today.

Settlers from other European countries also moved to South Carolina in search of a new life. People of German origin have been farming in the Orangeburg and Amelia regions since the early 1600s. Their farming practices helped them produce so much wheat that the area became known as the Breadbasket of South Carolina. Today, about one in ten South Carolinians is of German descent.

Another group of South Carolinians is of French origin. South Carolina had the largest French population of any of the original thirteen colonies. Many of these settlers were French Protestants known as Huguenots. They suffered persecution in Catholic France but had religious freedom in South Carolina. They found work as carpenters, cobblers, tailors, and craftsmen, and held seats in the legislature. Their descendants can be found in different parts of the state today.

African American Majority

From 1720 until 1930, the majority of South Carolina's population was black, primarily the descendants of former slaves. Beginning around 1910 and continuing through the 1970s, many African Americans in the South moved to the northern states or westward to escape the pervasive discrimination and prejudice they lived under. Most moved to big cities in the North. This large-scale movement was known as the Great Migration. In the 1980s and 1990s, this trend began to reverse, with many African Americans living in Northern states moving back down to the South. Some were following new economic opportunities. Others were rejoining family that had stayed behind.

Today, close to one-third of all South Carolinians are African American, and many are descended from enslaved people. Slaves who worked on the islands off South Carolina's eastern coast had little contact with their owners, who lived mostly on the mainland while overseers ran the plantation. Left to themselves, the slaves developed and preserved a culture based on African traditions. These people were called the Gullahs.

At the start of the Civil War, Union troops occupied the Sea Islands, freeing the slaves there. Most chose to remain on the islands, farming the land for Northern investors. The Gullahs continued to live and work there. To this day, they keep alive their fishing, weaving, storytelling, and music traditions. From bells and rattles to xylophones and one-string fiddles, Gullah music is full of traditional rhythms and styles.

The Gullahs have preserved many traditions and skills, such as basket weaving.

The Gullah even have their own language, a creole, or a blended language that is based on English but makes use of many **loan words** from African languages, and which also sometimes uses the grammatical structure of some African languages. The language is called Gullah or Geechee. Geechee is also another name for the Gullah people. A similar creole language is also spoken in the Bahamas.

About 250,000 people now speak Gullah in South Carolina and Georgia. Most also speak Standard

American English, too. Though there was historically some prejudice against the Gullah language, today many speak it as an emblem of pride in their culture and heritage. Most people know at least one Gullah word because it is featured in a well-known song often sung around campfires. *Kumbayah* is Gullah for "come by here."

The growth of tourism and the development of luxury resorts have put pressure on the Gullah way of life. With the help of such organizations as the Sea Islands Preservation Project, the Gullahs are working to protect their land and culture and encourage balanced development.

Other African Americans in the state are descended from slaves who were brought to the South Carolina mainland. Some come from immigrant families who left Africa or other parts of the world later on, or from families that moved into the state from different parts of the country. Regardless of their origins, African Americans are a vital part of South Carolina communities and businesses.

Hispanic and Asian Americans

Though many South Carolinians have roots in the state that go back for generations, newcomers have contributed to the state's growth in recent decades. They come from all parts of the world, including Asia and Mexico, and from other Spanish-speaking regions in Central America, South America, and the Caribbean.

The Hispanic, or Latino, population in South Carolina is fairly small, but it has been growing. Some Hispanics are migrant workers who come to the United States—perhaps temporarily and sometimes without having obtained permission to enter the country—to earn money to send back home. They often work very hard harvesting crops for low pay. Outreach groups and special programs have been set up to help these migrant workers and their families. Recently, many have gained increased rights and protection. Other Latinos are American citizens who have moved recently from Spanish-speaking countries or have lived in South Carolina for years. Hispanics are an active and important part of the state's industries, government, and educational system.

The Asian American population in South Carolina is small, but immigrants continue to move to the state from countries such as China, Japan, South Korea, the Philippines, and India. The Asian population of South Carolina is about 1.5 percent, much lower than the national average of 5.3 percent. Some Asian communities hold traditional celebrations during the year. Restaurants and stores specializing in Asian food and other products are becoming more common in different parts of the state.

The beautiful beaches attract many people to South Carolina.

Religions of South Carolinians

Historically, many people settled in the New World in search of religious freedom. Today, the majority of South Carolina residents (93 percent) identify themselves as Christian, with 84 percent being Protestant. Of the Protestants, 45 percent are Southern Baptists, 15 percent are Methodists, 5 percent are Presbyterian, and 19 percent identify as other Protestants. About 7 percent of the population is Roman Catholic, with a further 1 percent identifying as other Christians. Only 1 percent identifies as being of a non-Christian religion. South Carolina has one of the lowest numbers of people who are non-religious, with about 5 percent of the population identifying as atheists. There are so many churches of different denominations in Charleston that it is known as the Holy City.

Why South Carolina?

People live in South Carolina for many reasons. The state's mild climate is an attraction, along with its sunny beaches, scenic countryside, and historical heritage. Some find work in cities such as Charleston, Columbia, Greenville, Sumter, and Myrtle Beach, and settle there or in nearby suburbs. Others live on farms that have been in their families for generations. The coastal and island communities are popular places to live as well as to visit. Many Americans from other parts of the country move there when they retire. As people continue to move to South Carolina, their cultures, traditions, and fresh ideas contribute to the state's growth and prosperity.

10 KEY EVENTS

Carolina Day

Carolina Cup

1. Carolina Day

On June 28, South Carolinians celebrate the 1776 American victory at the Battle of Fort Moultrie. At the fort itself, on Sullivan's Island, families can enjoy musket and artillery demonstrations, a children's program, and a band concert.

2. Carolina Cup

A steeplechase for thoroughbred racehorses, the Carolina Cup is held in the spring, drawing sixty thousand people to Springdale Race Course in Camden. The National Steeplechase Museum is on the racecourse grounds, where the Colonial Cup steeplechase is also held, in autumn.

3. Governor's Annual Frog Jump Contest

Springfield hosts this event every year on the day before Easter. The winning frog goes on to California to represent South Carolina at the fabled Calaveras County Frog Jump. There is also a parade, arts and crafts, and other activities.

4. Lowcountry Oyster Festival

The World's Biggest Oyster Festival, featuring 80,000 pounds (36,287 kg) of oysters, is held in January at the Boone Hall Plantation in Mount Pleasant. It offers local food, oyster-eating and oyster-shucking contests, pony rides, and bounce houses.

5. The Original Gullah Festival

The Gullah Festival, held in Beaufort every Memorial Day weekend, celebrates the culture of the Gullah people. Along with music and food, this family-friendly event has storytelling, basket weaving, and demonstrations of other Gullah skills.

SOUTH CAROLINA

6. Pageland Watermelon Festival

This festival, held in Chesterfield County in July, is one of the oldest in South Carolina. The first celebration was held in 1951. With a parade, seed-spitting contest, beauty pageant, amusement rides, and concerts, the festival celebrates Pageland's heritage as an agrarian community.

7. South Carolina State Fair

Dating from 1839, the state fair is held in Columbia each year in October. There are farm animal competitions, displays of student art, concerts, and carnival rides.

8. Southern 500

Darlington Raceway, which was established in 1950, hosts this event on the NASCAR Sprint Cup Series in September. In addition to the big race, there are events in other car classifications, a parade, and concerts.

9. Spoleto Festival USA

Jazz, choral, symphonic, opera, and chamber music fills Charleston for seventeen days and nights each spring. This celebration of culture also attracts theater and dance groups. All of them perform in the city's historic theaters, churches, and in open spaces.

10. World Grits Festival

In the 1980s, it was discovered that the people in St. George ate more grits per capita than anyone anywhere else in the world. This led to the festival, which every April features a Rolling-in-the-Grits contest, as well as grits-grinding demonstrations, gospel music, and a parade.

South Carolina State Fair

World Grits Festival

Charleston City Hall was completed in 1804 and is open for tours.

How the Government Works

R unning a state requires a lot of hard work from many people. At the local level, towns and cities have their own governments. They handle matters that affect the town or city, such as zoning and police and fire protection. On the next level are the state's forty-six county governments. Each one handles matters that affect the county as a whole.

The State Constitution

The primary document that lays out the government of South Carolina is the state constitution. The state has had many constitutions; the first one was approved in 1776. The current constitution was first drafted in 1895. There have been significant changes to the state's constitution over the years, allowing the state to adapt to changing times. For example, some sections of earlier versions of the constitution set limits on who could vote. People had to prove themselves worthy by passing tests on the articles of the state constitution, in addition to reading and writing tests. They also had to own a certain amount of property in order to vote. This kept many people from voting, and the constitution was later changed to expand voting rights.

Today, any changes to the state constitution have to be approved by two-thirds of the members of each legislative house, as well as voted for by the public. After that, it still has to be ratified by the majority of each of the legislative houses. An amendment that is not ratified is not passed, even if the public overwhelmingly voted for it.

State Government

The state government deals with issues relating to the whole state. Like the federal government, it is made up of three branches: the executive, the legislative, and the judicial. Each branch has its own particular responsibilities.

Columbia is the state capital. Located near the center of South Carolina, it is the city where most state officials work and where the legislature meets. The governor's mansion is located there.

The state government of South Carolina spends more than $20 billion a year. More than 40 percent of the money is used for health care and social services, and about 35 percent is spent on education.

Where does the state get its money? About 60 percent of the state revenue comes from state taxes and fees. These include the sales taxes on items that people buy and the state income taxes that citizens and companies must pay depending on how much money they earn. The 6 percent state sales tax is used solely to support education. Other money used by the state comes from the federal government.

Branches of Government

Executive

The governor supervises the state government, plans the budget, appoints certain officials, and approves or rejects bills that are passed by the legislature. He or she serves a four-year term and cannot serve more than two terms in a row. Voters elect a total of nine executive officers. In addition to the governor, these include the Lieutenant Governor, Secretary of State, Attorney General, Adjutant General, Commissioner of Agriculture, Comptroller General,

Drop That Eel!

In South Carolina, it is illegal to buy, sell, or possess an electric eel. That is mostly to prevent the nonnative species from escaping into local waters, but the law also protects anyone silly enough to think an electric eel might make a cool pet. The same goes for piranhas. It is also, incidentally, illegal to electrocute fish, whether or not the fish themselves are electric.

The inside of the South Carolina State House was renovated in the 1990s.

State Treasurer, and the Superintendent of Education. Those who hold these offices also serve four-year terms.

Legislative

Members of this branch belong to the state legislature, which is called the general assembly. They make the state's laws and must approve a state budget each year. The general assembly is bicameral, which means it is divided into two houses, or chambers. The upper house, or senate, has 46 members elected to four-year terms. The lower house, or house of representatives, has 124 members, elected to two-year terms. There is no limit on the number of terms that legislators may serve. Their meeting place is the South Carolina State House.

Judicial

The Supreme Court is the highest court in the state. Elected by the general assembly, its five justices serve ten-year terms. The state Supreme Court reviews decisions made by lower-level state courts and can decide whether or not a state law agrees with the state constitution. Beneath the Supreme Court is the court of appeals, with ten judges elected to six-year terms. The court of appeals can review decisions made by lower courts that hold trials. These lower courts include family court, which handles divorce, custody, adoption, and other family matters, as well as juvenile justice. There is also the circuit court, which has both a civil and a criminal division.

Representatives In Congress

Voters in South Carolina elect lawmakers to represent them in the US Congress in Washington, DC. Like all other states, South Carolina has two US senators. The number of members a state can elect to the United States House of Representatives is based on its population in the latest census. After the 2010 Census, South Carolina was entitled to seven seats in the United States House of Representatives.

How a Bill Becomes a Law

When the general assembly is meeting, any member of the state senate or state house of representatives can propose a new law and try to get it passed. A proposed law is called a bill. A bill introduced by a senator is first considered in the senate, and a bill proposed by a representative is first considered in the house. The bill is read out loud and then sent to a committee of lawmakers. Their job is to examine the bill carefully, perhaps make a few changes to it, and then either accept or reject it. If a majority of the committee votes to accept the bill, it goes to the full chamber for consideration, possible further changes, and then a vote.

If a majority of the members of one chamber vote to accept a version of the bill, it is sent to the other house, where the process of considering and voting on the bill is repeated. The second chamber may make changes to the bill it received before passing it. In that case, the bill usually goes to a special committee (called a conference committee), made up of members from each house, who agree on a final version of the bill. This final version must then be passed again by both houses.

When both houses have passed the bill in exactly the same form, it goes to the governor. The governor can accept and sign the bill, in which case it becomes a law. The bill also becomes a law if the governor takes no action on it for five days. The governor may also reject (veto) the bill. In order for a vetoed bill to become a law, two-thirds of the members in each house must then vote for it.

In Their Own Words

"I encourage people to find and use the power of their voices just as much when I do not agree with those voices as when I do agree with them."
–Governor Nikki Haley

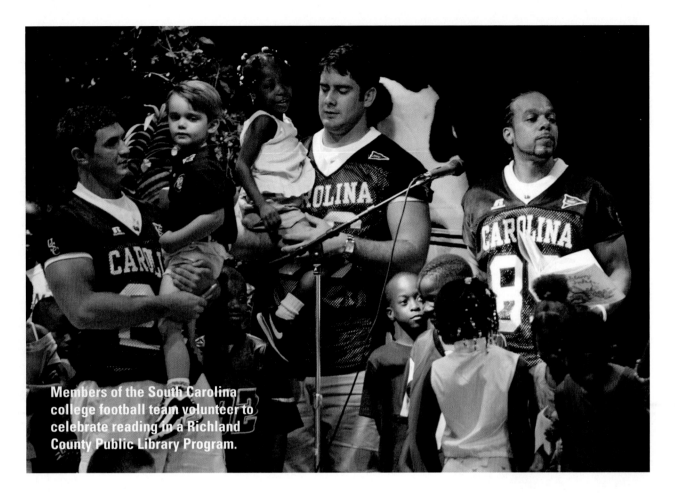

Members of the South Carolina college football team volunteer to celebrate reading in a Richland County Public Library Program.

What You Can Do

When you get to the age of eighteen, you will be able to vote in local, state, and national elections. In the meantime, it is a good idea to learn about what is going on in your state. Newspapers and television news programs can help you understand important issues and learn more about the people who represent you. You can also contact these representatives about issues that concern you.

There are other ways to make a difference in your community. In South Carolina, as in other states, children and adults can volunteer in their communities. You may be able to help out at a local charity, animal shelter, food kitchen, or a home for the elderly. Wherever you see a problem in your state, there is probably something you can do to help by giving your time and attention.

One of the shining stars of South Carolina's volunteer programs is PalmettoPride. This nonprofit organization has won awards for its work in keeping the Palmetto State clean by promoting recycling and the reduction of litter. The organization's website offers kid-friendly activities and details about joining or setting up a litter initiative.

POLITICAL FIGURES

FROM SOUTH CAROLINA

★ John C. Calhoun: Vice President, 1825-1832

This seventh vice president of the United States and South Carolina native was also a senator (1845–1850), secretary of state, and secretary of war. He supported states' rights over the will of the central US government and was in favor of continued slavery in the South.

★ Nikki Haley: Governor, 2011-

Nikki Haley was born in Bamberg. Her parents were immigrants from India who developed a successful clothing company. Elected in 2004 to the state house of representatives, she was the first Indian American to win public office in South Carolina. In 2010, she was elected the 116th governor of the state.

★ Strom Thurmond: US Senator, 1954-2003

Born in Edgefield in 1902, Strom Thurmond served as governor of South Carolina for four years and as a US senator for forty-eight years. He began his career as a Democrat and ended as a Republican. The World War II veteran fought against the Civil Rights Act of 1957, but later he held many leadership positions.

SOUTH CAROLINA
YOU CAN MAKE A DIFFERENCE

Contacting Lawmakers

To find out who your legislators in South Carolina are and how to contact them, go to **www.scstatehouse.gov**. Locate the "Find Your Legislators" link on the bottom of the page. Once you type your address in, you will find out who represents you in both the state and the federal government. There are also links to each elected official's voting record so you can see where they stand on issues that matter to you. There is also a drop-down box you can use to contact any of the state legislators.

Video Evidence

Usually, the public has to rely on officers' statements and witnesses to find out what happened during a law enforcement action. Sometimes the truth can get distorted, either by the officer or by the suspect. A bill that would help remedy that problem was proposed in South Carolina. It called for all law enforcement officers to wear body-mounted cameras that would record their activities. That bill seemed unlikely to pass until the April 4, 2015 shooting death of Walter Scott.

Citizens protesting the death of Walter Scott helped bring about a state law.

A law enforcement officer shot the unarmed Walter Scott in the back as he was running away. The officer claimed that Scott had tried to get his Taser, and that he shot Scott in self-defense. However, a bystander took a video of the incident that showed something different. Scott didn't appear to ever grab the officer's Taser, and later it looked like an officer planted the Taser near Scott's body. The officer was later charged with murder.

Outrage over this incident led people to support the use of police body cameras. That way, they hoped, the truth of every incident could be captured on video. Civil rights leaders called for calm, and protests were held peacefully. On June 10, 2015, a law was passed requiring all South Carolina law enforcement agencies to use body cameras. South Carolina is the first state to pass a body camera law.

South Carolina workers assemble Boeing 787 Dreamliners at a plant that opened in 2011.

Making a Living

South Carolinians make a living in many different ways. Some work as farmers or fishers, and many more work in factories or in the construction industry. But the largest number of workers, by far, provides services to other people or businesses instead of producing a product. The service industry includes people working in education, health care, wholesale or retail business, and the government, among other fields. Many service workers in South Carolina have jobs at one of the military bases in the state. Others work at the docks in Charleston, where cargo ships from all over the world load and unload.

Tourism

About thirty million people visit South Carolina each year. Visitors flock to the resorts along the coast in spring and summer. It was at the resort of Myrtle Beach that the popular state dance, the Carolina Shag, got its name in the 1930s. There are shag-dancing festivals held along the coast throughout the year. In addition, the many state parks, and Congaree National Park, provide opportunities for hiking, biking, canoeing, and camping. The state's lakes, rivers, and streams draw boaters and fishers throughout the year.

Fun, sun, and fishing draw vacationers to South Carolina's coast.

People also come to South Carolina to enjoy its historic beauty. Since South Carolina was one of the thirteen original colonies, it has a long and rich history. Historic buildings, plantations, and battlefields are open to the public. Among the favorite spots is Charleston's Historic District, which includes Rainbow Row. This is a section of thirteen restored row houses painted in the pastel colors of the Caribbean. South Carolina offers many ways to learn about the history of the state as well as the country. South Carolina is also home to many museums and theaters.

Farming and Fishing

Field crops such as cotton were once the biggest moneymakers for South Carolina. Although agriculture is much less important now, it remains a vital part of the economy. The chief sources of farm income today include chickens, greenhouse and nursery products, turkeys, cattle, and dairy products. South Carolina farmers also grow corn, soybeans, wheat, tobacco, hay, watermelons, apples, peanuts, and pecans. Cotton is still grown in some counties. The Palmetto State also produces more peaches than any other state except California.

Seafood is a popular South Carolina product. Shrimp, crabs, oysters, and clams are harvested on the coast. Ocean fish are also important. Fresh seafood is served in restaurants throughout the state. It is also shipped to other states.

Manufacturing

Manufacturing now brings in about one-sixth of the state's income. Leading products include automobiles and other transportation equipment. Textile manufacturing has declined but remains important. South Carolina's factories turn out cotton, silk, wool, polyester, acrylics, and nylon. Some factories make the fabric into clothes.

South Carolina also has a productive chemical industry. Factories across the state manufacture chemicals for fertilizers used on farms in South Carolina and other states. In addition to manufacturing useful products, the factories provide jobs for South Carolinians.

The federal government also brings money into the state. There are several military bases in South Carolina. The Savannah River Site removes nuclear material from decommissioned weapons and serves as a nuclear storage facility. The Department of Defense also uses this site for other nuclear research.

Like other states, South Carolina has lost many manufacturing jobs in recent years. The state is relying more and more on job growth in other parts of the economy to help create opportunities for workers in the years ahead.

WE "FINISH" ON TIME

2,8,3 DAYS SINCE THE LAST LATE ORDER

Textiles are still an important part of the state's manufacturing industry.

10 KEY INDUSTRIES

Golf

Peaches

1. Automotive Manufacturing

There are more than 250 automotive manufacturing plants in the state, which has become a national leader in this industry. BMW opened a plant in Spartanburg in 1992, and Honda opened one in Timmonsville in 1998. Volvo plans to open a plant in Charleston in 2018.

2. Cattle and Dairy

South Carolina has five milk-processing plants that in 2011 produced 32 million gallons (121,133,177 liters) of milk. Some of that milk was turned into butter or cheese. The state beef cattle industry generates about $140 million each year.

3. Golf

People from all over the United States travel to South Carolina to play golf on the state's excellent courses. Each year, close to two million rounds are played in the Myrtle Beach area and another one million in Hilton Head.

4. Peaches

Among the fifty states, South Carolina ranks second in overall peach production. The South Carolina Peach Festival is held every July in Gaffney. The town's water tower looks like a huge peach.

5. Pecans

Georgia sometimes gets all the attention for both peaches and pecans, but both are produced in great numbers in South Carolina. The state cultivates thousands of bountiful pecan trees, and foreign demand for pecans makes the nuts worth more than $3 a pound.

6. Poultry

Farmers produce poultry products, including eggs, tiny Cornish game hens, chickens, and turkeys. Most of South Carolina's livestock income comes from poultry farms.

7. Textiles

Historically, textile manufacturing was the state's biggest industry. Though it declined, there has been a recent upswing. Products include diapers, mops, cleaning wipes, wool, thread, and furniture upholstery.

8. Timber

Trees cover about two-thirds of the state and contribute to South Carolina's beauty. Timber is the state's most important crop. The timber industry provides more than thirty thousand jobs.

9. Tobacco

About 250 South Carolina farmers contract with big tobacco companies to plant more than 15,000 acres (6,070 hectares) of tobacco each year, producing a total revenue of about $56 million. Though tobacco production has declined around the country, it is still an important state crop.

10. Tourism

This is one of the largest industries in the state. People come to relax at the beach, visit Charleston's Historic District, or tour many of the sprawling plantations that once flourished in South Carolina and have been preserved and renovated. They also hike on up-country trails.

Poultry

Tourism

Recipe for South Carolina Peach Pecan Pie Smoothie

Georgia might call itself the Peach State, but really South Carolina produces many more peaches than its neighbor to the south. South Carolina also produces a bumper crop of tasty pecans. This easy-to-make smoothie captures the flavor of a classic peach-pecan pie in a healthy smoothie.

Frozen peaches work best because they make the smoothie frosty without diluting the flavor. If you prefer to use fresh or canned peaches, you can either freeze the sliced peaches for an hour or two before use or add about five ice cubes to the smoothie when blending.

This recipe can be adapted to your tastes. You can add more or less sugar or use honey or maple syrup to sweeten it. You can use skim or low-fat milk, or soy or almond milk. Change the spices to taste.

What You Need

1 cup (237 milliliters) frozen peaches

1 ripe banana

½ cup (118 mL) milk

½ cup (118 mL) vanilla yogurt

¼ cup (59 mL) pecans

1 teaspoon (4.9 mL) brown sugar

¼ teaspoon (1.2 mL) cinnamon

⅛ teaspoon (.6 mL) nutmeg

What To Do

- Add all ingredients to a blender. Begin on the lowest setting and gradually work your way up to the highest setting. Blend for about twenty seconds on the highest setting. Makes two servings.

State Money

A state's prosperity can be measured in many different ways. South Carolina's gross state product is a measure of how much economic output the state generates with all of its businesses. In 1997, South Carolina's gross state product was $97 billion. A decade later, in 2007, the gross state product had climbed to $153 billion.

Jobs and Income

The average yearly income per person is $23,943, which is about $4,000 less than the national average. The recession in the late 2000s hit South Carolina and the rest of America hard, resulting in a dramatic increase in unemployment. In November and December 2009, unemployment in the state hit the lowest point at 12 percent. Since then the economy has improved, and as of May 2015, the unemployment rate was 6.8 percent. This was well above the national average of 5.5 percent

South Carolina is known as a "right to work" state. That means that South Carolina has laws that regulate agreements between labor unions and employers, which say that an employer cannot exclude anyone from possible hiring based on whether they have joined a union or other group, or paid any dues to any organization. There are twenty-five right-to-work states.

In 2007, there were 360,397 firms operating in South Carolina. These were owned by a diverse group of people. African Americans own 12.1 percent of those firms. Hispanics owned 1.7 percent of those firms, and Asians owned 1.8 percent. In that same year, women owned 27.6 percent of the firms.

Foreign Investment

South Carolina is home to approximately 1,950 firms that are owned by foreign interests. Together, those companies employ about 135,000 people, adding to the overall economy of the state. In 2010, foreign investment contributed a significant amount to the South Carolina economy—around $1 billion.

One of the biggest foreign investors is the car company BMW, which has a factory in Spartanburg. It opened in 1994. There, workers manufacture about six hundred vehicles every day. In 2010, the company said that it would commit $750 million to improve and expand the factory. When the work is complete, the Spartanburg factory will have the largest number of employees of any car factory in the country. It will have an estimated output of 240,000 cars every year. These luxury cars will be sold both in the United States and in Europe. The South Carolina ports get a boost from any export by ship.

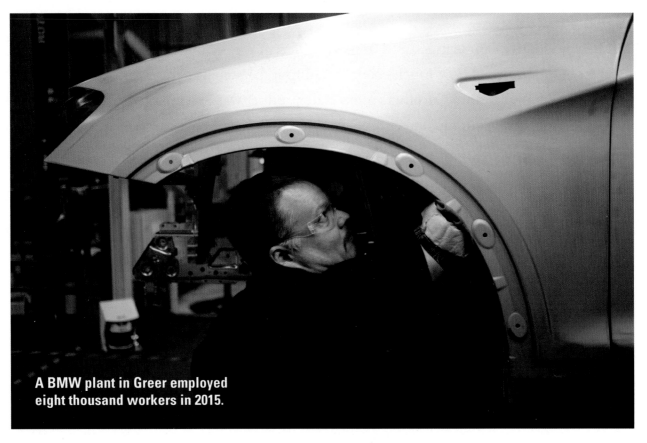

A BMW plant in Greer employed eight thousand workers in 2015.

New Investors

South Carolina is attracting new companies all of the time. In November 2011, the airplane manufacturer Boeing opened a factory for making commercial airplanes in Charleston. It is one of the largest employers in the state. When ground was broken on the new site in 2009, it lifted spirits because it came near the end of the recession of the late 2000s. Residents knew that the factory would provide jobs and help improve the economy. Boeing originally planned to create some 3,800 jobs. In return, the state offered a package of incentives, such as tax breaks, worth about $900 million. It was thought that the investment Boeing was making in the state made those concessions worthwhile. The factory primarily assembles and delivers the new Boeing 787 Dreamliner. This twin-engine, midsize, commercial airplane is then sold to buyers around the world.

Boeing started construction on a decorative paint plant at its Charleston facility in 2014, and it was set to open in 2016. As of June 2015, the company employed 7,792 people in the state.

Finding a Balance

Historically, a great deal of the South Carolina economy has depended on the land and the water. The textile manufacturing industry depended on the vast production of cotton. The

South Carolina's climate allows for a long golf season.

huge lumber industry, as well as the related manufacture of paper from wood pulp, relies not only on the state's forests but on its waterways. Formerly, waterpower ran mills. Today, it provides hydroelectric power and of course waters the state's many crops and timberland.

Excessive farming has damaged some parts of state land, and in other areas, forests have been cleared for farms and homes. Overuse of fertilizer has damaged once-pristine waterways. Now, South Carolina depends on its natural beauty to attract tourists—a huge part of the economy—and must make an effort to preserve its plants, animals, waterways, and wild places.

Over the past few decades, as the population has grown, more land has been developed to make room for roadways and shopping centers. Heavy development in parts of the Sea Islands has crowded out natural habitats for egrets, alligators, and rare bird species. Also of concern to many is the storage of nuclear wastes at the Savannah River Site, not far from major cities in South Carolina and Georgia.

In 1989, the South Carolina Environmental Excellence Program (SCEEP) was set up. Companies and organizations that join this program agree to try to improve the environment by preventing pollution and conserving energy and other resources. In order to create jobs, businesses need to grow. At the same time, it is up to everybody to care for and respect the land.

SOUTH CAROLINA
STATE MAP

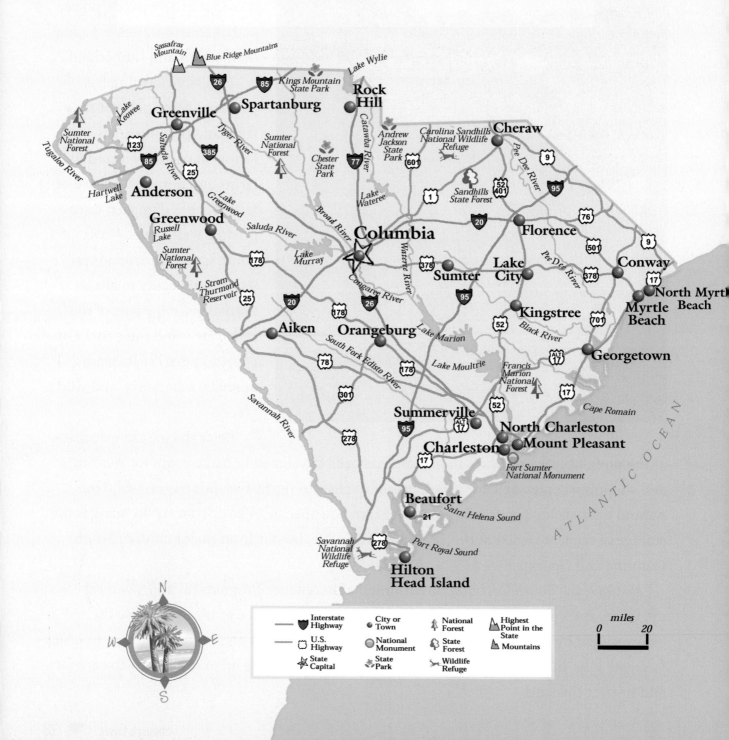

Sassafras Mountain
Blue Ridge Mountains
Lake Wylie
Kings Mountain State Park
26
85
Greenville
Spartanburg
Rock Hill
Cheraw
9
Lake Keowee
Sumter National Forest
Andrew Jackson State Park
Carolina Sandhills National Wildlife Refuge
Pee Dee River
Tugaloo River
123
Saluda River
Tyger River
Sumter National Forest
601
52
401
95
85
25
385
Chester State Park
77
Catawba River
1
Sandhills State Forest
76
Hartwell Lake
Anderson
Lake Waterre
20
Florence
501
9
Greenwood
Lake Greenwood
Saluda River
Broad River
Lake Waterre
Columbia
Pee Dee River
Conway
17
Russell Lake
Sumter National Forest
Lake Murray
378
Sumter
Lake City
378
North Myrtle Beach
J. Strom Thurmond Reservoir
178
Congaree River
Waterre River
95
Kingstree
701
Myrtle Beach
25
20
Aiken
Orangeburg
178
Lake Marion
52
Black River
Georgetown
78
South Fork Edisto River
178
Lake Moultrie
ALT 17
17
301
Francis Marion National Forest
Cape Romain
Savannah River
278
Summerville
95
ALT 17
52
North Charleston
Mount Pleasant
Charleston
17
Fort Sumter National Monument
ATLANTIC OCEAN
Beaufort
21
Saint Helena Sound
Savannah National Wildlife Refuge
278
Port Royal Sound
Hilton Head Island

N
W E
S

	Interstate Highway	City or Town	National Forest	Highest Point in the State
	U.S. Highway	National Monument	State Forest	Mountains
	State Capital	State Park	Wildlife Refuge	

miles
0   20

SOUTH CAROLINA
MAP SKILLS

1. What national wildlife refuge is at the mouth of the Savannah River?

2. What city, also the state capital, is located along Interstates 20 and 26?

3. What national forest stretches along the northern segment of South Carolina's western border?

4. What island, a popular tourist destination, is located at the southern tip of South Carolina, near its border with Georgia?

5. What lake, located to the northwest of Lake Moultrie, is the largest lake in South Carolina?

6. The Broad and the Saluda Rivers merge near the state capital to form what major river?

7. What coastal city is located where the Black and the Pee Dee Rivers meet the Atlantic Ocean?

8. What lake is located to the north of Rock Hill?

9. What national monument is located near the cities of Charleston, North Charleston, and Mount Pleasant?

10. What ocean lies along South Carolina's southeastern coast?

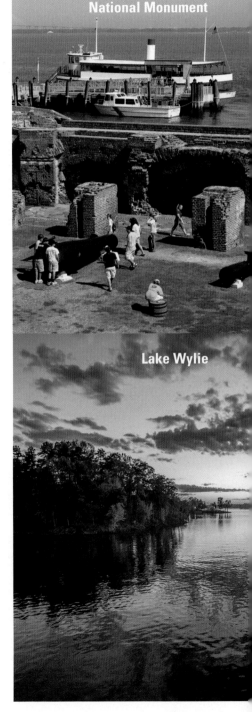

Fort Sumter National Monument

Lake Wylie

1. Savannah National Wildlife Refuge
2. Columbia
3. Sumter National Forest
4. Hilton Head Island
5. Lake Marion
6. Congaree River
7. Georgetown
8. Lake Wylie
9. Fort Sumter National Monument
10. Atlantic Ocean

State Flag, Seal, and Song

The state flag of South Carolina was adopted in 1861. It is blue with a palmetto tree and a silver crescent. Blue is the color of the uniforms worn by the soldiers who fought in the American Revolution. The crescent looks like the symbol on the soldiers' hats. The palmetto tree represents the colonists' victory over the British at Sullivan's Island in 1776. The left side of the seal has a palmetto tree growing from a fallen oak tree. This also represents the defeat of the British at Sullivan's Island. The left side also shows the dates for South Carolina's first constitution (March 26, 1776) and for the Declaration of Independence (July 4, 1776). The right side of the seal shows a woman who symbolizes hope triumphing over danger. The state's two mottos surround the two ovals. On the left are the Latin words *Animis Opibusque Parati*, meaning "Prepared in Mind and Resources." On the right, *Dum Spiro Spero* is Latin for "While I Breathe, I Hope."

The state song is "Carolina." It is based on a poem by Henry Timrod and was set to music by Anne Custis Burgess. It became the official state song in 1911. In 1984, a second state song, "South Carolina on my Mind," was also designated.

To read the lyrics of and to listen to both songs, visit **www.sciway.net/facts/songs.html**

Glossary

blockade Closing or sealing a place, usually along water, to keep people or supplies from entering or leaving.

civil rights The basic rights of all citizens to be treated equally without regard to race, gender, religion, or other considerations.

delta The place where a river or rivers empty into an ocean or sea.

ecoregion An ecosystem that is in a particular geographic area, with a uniform climate.

hydroelectric Making energy or electricity using water as a power source.

immunity Having antibodies or other internal means of resisting infections from bacteria, viruses, or toxins.

loan words A word borrowed from a language and made part of the receiving language without being translated.

Loyalists People who supported Britain and the king during the American Revolutionary War.

palmetto One of several species of small fan palms native to the Southeast.

Patriots People who supported the colonists and desired freedom from English control during the American Revolutionary War.

secede To withdraw from membership in a group or federal union.

slavery Keeping human beings as if they were property, forcing them to work and denying them of human rights.

timber Wood that is for use in carpentry, house building, etc.; or trees that are grown to make that wood.

Trail of Tears The brutal route many Native Americans were forced to travel from the southeast to new territory west of the Mississippi River under the Indian Removal Act.

More About South Carolina

BOOKS

Harmon, Daniel S. *South Carolina: Past and Present*. New York: Rosen Publishing, 2010.

Higgins, David R. *The Swamp Fox: Francis Marion's Campaign in the Carolinas 1780*. Oxford, England: Osprey Publishing, 2013.

Jerome, Kate Boehm. *Charleston, SC: Cool Stuff Every Kid Should Know*. Mount Pleasant, SC: Arcadia Publishing, 2008.

Mis, Melody S. *The Colony of South Carolina: A Primary Source History*. New York: Rosen Publishing, 2006.

WEBSITES

Official Website of the State of South Carolina

www.sc.gov

South Carolina Agriculture Kids' Page

www.sc.gov/residents/Agriculture/Pages/kidsPages.aspx

South Carolina Tourism Official Site

www.discoversouthcarolina.com

ABOUT THE AUTHORS

Debra Hess has written dozens of books for children, including *Wilson Sat Alone*. She has also written for an award-winning children's television series.

William McGeveran, a former editor at World Almanac Books, is now a freelance writer and editor.

Laura L. Sullivan is the author of more than thirty fiction and nonfiction books for children and co-wrote the romantic mystery *Girl About Town* with Adam Shankman.

Index

Page numbers in **boldface** are illustrations. Entries in **boldface** are glossary terms.

Index